D1565780

CYBORG
SISTER

CYBORG SISTER

Jackie Craven

FINALIST FOR THE CHARLOTTE MEW PRIZE

HEADMISTRESS PRESS

ISBN 978-1-7358236-6-9

Cover art: © 1980 Louise Craven Hourrigan, Venus and the Half-Shell. Oil on Masonite, 32" x 16"

PUBLISHER
Headmistress Press
60 Shipview Lane
Sequim, WA 98382
Telephone: 917-428-8312
Email: headmistresspress@gmail.com
Website: headmistresspress.blogspot.com

CONTENTS

Quietly at the Top of the Stairs   1

She Never Answers My Knock   5

Boys Scuttle Between the Walls   6

Horticulture Magazine Lists the Most Resilient Roses   7

Our House Is Menstruating   8

Every Day, Her Steel Frame Expands   9

Wings Throb Overhead   10

She Tries to Hide the Oily Scent of Her Maturation   11

Dusk Lands on Page 37 of The Whispering Statue   12

Anthuriums Slink Through the Back Door   13

I Cross-Examine the Microwave   15

Lies Lie on the Lawn   16

A Tadpole Gets in the Municipal Pool   17

Our Father Gives Us Robotic Roses   18

When her Tongue Breaks, My Sister Tries to Say   19

BuzzFuse Lists the World's Most Extraordinary Women   20

No One Speaks of the Empty Ghosts in the Basement Closet   21

In My Mirror   22

Under Anesthesia I Remember a Watermelon with Slippery Seeds   23

About the Author   25

Acknowledgements   27

QUIETLY AT THE TOP OF THE STAIRS

— two rooms sit back-to-back and pretend to be content. And so they should be, pillows soft as milkweed, rumpled books tousled in floral sheets. One room, drowsy as honeysuckle, has *The Best of Nancy Drew.* The other has a tattered copy of *Frankenstein.* August presses against leaded glass. Curtains wilt in the heat. Behind each latched door — a shush of turning pages. Where to go, how to disappear. Can a room survive without its walls? Neither tells the other ...

SHE NEVER ANSWERS MY KNOCK

Older than me and too iridescent to leave her room,
my sister clicks and hums through the night.
I want to crack the door and touch the edge
of her secrets. She eats shadows in bed. If I close
my eyes, I can feel a chitter and thrum of gears,
each one small as a baby's tooth.

So much artistry went into her construction —
tweezers trembling in swaying light,
Mama breathing *careful, careful,*
Daddy weaving magnificent intestinal springs.

He designed the manifold, but it was Mama
who wrapped the wires and tied them
into durable knots.

Boys Scuttle Between the Walls

they   slip   under doors   shhh
they're here   we cover   our heads
they follow   us inside   swarm
our eyes   buzz   our ears   stink the air
give us   sweaters&rings   give us
lockets&photos   give us   snips
of hair   we try   the stairs   every floor
zzzzzzz   they're here   boysss
in the halls   boysss   in the yard
boysss   at the pool   lifeboy   sits high
watches   from high   preying man-tis
legs   preying   man-tis   arms
quick   Mama says   show him
your teeth   show him   your smile

HORTICULTURE MAGAZINE LISTS
THE MOST RESILIENT ROSES

Ivory Saboteurs. Alabaster Knights— We know their names
because we hid inside the garden shed and watched
our father slice open the hips.

He bioengineered each seed— designed the hybrid pistils,
the translucent thorns, every detail perfect,
especially the *Atomic Pearls.* He loves these the best, but

they are the ones who tromp through the daylilies
and pluck out their tongues. No one can contain
his creations— They burst through the garden gate

and consume Amaryllis along the highway. My sister,
my cultivated sister, knows exactly what to say:
That's alright, Daddy. You'll do better next time.

I'm a creeping Mugwort. She's his *Crimson Joy.*

Our House Is Menstruating

Being unclean, we send our refrigerator to a mountain retreat
for counseling and quiet meditation.

Being unclean, we feed the drains a gentle solution of mineral oil
and medicinal cannabis.

Mama asks our doctor to prescribe something stronger
for the microwave.

She writes to *Ask Heloise,* who suggests mayonnaise
with a splash of vinegar.

We treat the curtains to a permanent wave.
Give the blinds permission to spend all day at the spa.

Being unclean, we copulate the rooms with a Dirt Devil
stretch hose and extension wand.

Mama says cleanliness requires perseverance
and hard plastic tools.

EVERY DAY, HER STEEL FRAME EXPANDS

When her skin stretches tight, my sister
writhes and tries to smile. She can't help

screeching at the knees.

Give her time, Daddy says.
She'll calibrate.

She rests in the sun-drenched garden
and sips Castrol with a sprig of mint.

Fibers unravel at the wrists.

It's impossible to ignore
the whine of straining wires.

*You should've known our daughter
would need zippers,* Mama sighs,

and tears my sister open at the seams.

WINGS THROB OVERHEAD

—Heavy flocks swooping low,
                perching on telephone wires,
        shrieking and cawing our names.

        Don't look, Sister says,
you'll encourage them,
                but how can I ignore the hunger

that follows us home from school?
                As though by accident, a ruffled one
        bumps against my chest.

Another grazes my neck.
                I sense them behind curtains
        and in the stairwell where I find

my sister—my careful, proper sister—
                eyes glazed, feathers pressed
        to her cheek. I think surely

the beak will draw blood
                but she sways with such pleasure,
        my own lips sting and glow.

She says I'm too young
                to understand, but
        at night I hug my pillow

and smell their down.
                They like me best.

SHE TRIES TO HIDE THE OILY SCENT OF HER MATURATION

Behind her bedroom door, the ssss of Shalimar
spritzed from cut glass bottles and, at night,
the hiss of my sister unzipping.

For a moment her membrane holds its shape,
elbows bent and hands folded in the posture
she wears at her desk in school. Then it crinkles down.

I imagine a perfect pointed toe stepping out,
careful not to snag cellulose threads.

What does she become
while she soaks herself in the bathroom sink?
Can a girl exist without a skin?

I find her folded over the shower curtain rod,
arms dangling, the mask of her face upside down,
dripping into the tub.

Dusk Lands on Page 37
of The Whispering Statue

— interrupting the moment when Nancy Drew
retrieves the waterlogged letter
that contains the telltale clue
that will lead to the haunted garden
and a devious sculptor. I want
to ride with Nancy on rattling trains
and crashing seaplanes, but here comes Dusk
like a suspicious caller, the likely leader
of a ring of thieves.

ANTHURIUMS SLINK THROUGH THE BACK DOOR

—They scuttle
     across the night kitchen,
giggle
     in dank corners,
breed.

     Dioxin does no good,
and just try to squash one
     inside a dictionary
or a Bible.

     Dead?
Not yet.

     Beneath my sister's bed,
the creeping epiphytes
     our father grew —

jiggling their cleavage,
     spraying pollen
from their spiny tongues.

     — Don't hurt them! They're mine.

My big sister,
     my sensible sister —
red-faced and bawling
     over a snickering nest
of anthuriums.

     She'll thank me someday,

but now—
>   how her sobs soar
above the rumble
>   of my vacuum.

How the dust bag swells with her rage.

I Cross-Examine the Microwave

When the display blinks 12:00
is it midnight or noon?
Which button will defrost my sweater?
Which button will explain my sister?

The carousel turns but where are the ponies?
Should I reset the timer to 2010?
How many years will fit in 2.2 cubic feet?
How many days of summer?

Every morning — The same gray face
pressed to the glass? Must I wait for a ring
before I open the door?

Will the touchpad read my fingerprints?
Will the MEMORY button remember my name?
Will my sister answer my call?
How long must I wait?

LIES LIE ON THE LAWN

like garden
hoses

stealthy stripes
sliding
through the grass

then twisting
and falsely
hissing

as though
bare toes
have no

eyes

although
of course
they do

my sister
says

A Tadpole Gets in
the Municipal Pool

Iridescent as oil   it swirls whirlpools

         bumps the painted wall   and flickers

beneath feathered shadows.   My head bobs

         blue ripples.   A blurry voice drifts

through chlorinated air —

         One kiss and you get a prince.

The tadpole paddles toward me

         and I'm like —   *Ugh, go away*

and I'm like —   *Must remember to smile*

         and I'm like —   *Today's my lucky day.*

So I open my mouth   I show him my teeth —

         Sister   I swallow him.

OUR FATHER GIVES US
ROBOTIC ROSES

Coiled hinges screech open,
        brass petals unfurl.
My rose purrs beneath the sepals—

        my sister's vibrates
like a Stratocaster guitar.
        Don't touch, she shrieks because

I ruin everything, but I'm the one
        who oils the steel thorns and
dusts the compressor coils

        and smells rubber gaskets overheating
and lovingly sets our father's electric gift
        in a cool basin of water.

Wire filaments spark; steam billows
        up the stairs where my sister explodes:
Nine joules but where did you put the coulomb?

        Her with her wet resin eyes.
Her with copper hair still damp
        from her afternoon shower.

Sputtering like a drowned toaster.

WHEN HER TONGUE BREAKS, MY SISTER TRIES TO SAY

They put me in   I want. You to know

they put.   Is you vay cay   tion.   Put me

onetwothree.   One nay   tion. I want you

to know. One two   station. They put me in

ice long. Do you know   they put me in salve

ation. Is you know   they put. I so you

to know they put me in. Sixseven   nay

tion. So long they put. Onetwo four   I want.

You to know they put me in I so lay

tion.   They put.   I want.

BuzzFuse Lists the World's Most Extraordinary Women

She soars seven feet two and tips the scale
at two pounds seven. Or, her legs are long

as telephone poles, thin as paper cuts. She wears
a lavender beard and the beard cascades to her toes

or she has no toes, only steel-capped knees
on which she runs marathons. Her tendons

bend backwards. She opens bottles
with her feet, or she breathes underwater,

or she swallows thirteen swords simultaneously.
When she opens her mouth, her tongue

unfurls like Rapunzel's hair. Boys try to climb it,
but they can't get past the world's longest fingernails

that spiral around her tower. Still, boys die trying
because the world's most extraordinary woman

has two heads and three breasts.
Medical professionals say her spine

will curve beneath the weight
of her exceptionalism.

But what are her options?

No One Speaks of the Empty Ghosts in the Basement Closet

Drooping from wire hangers and arranged
chronologically by age — my sister's discards
preserved in camphor and talcum powder.
Here's the deflated balloon of her infancy.
Here's a hollow snuggie with toes like blackeye peas
and here are skins with polished nails,
skins with ballerina feet, and the skin she wore
when she won the seventh grade spelling bee,
her back pressed to the wall so no one would see
the bulky zipper along her spine.

Yellow in the light of a pull-chain bulb,
they rustle at my touch and seem to whisper,
Stay away, but what's the harm in looking?
Her sixteenth skin is sheer as a butterfly net,
beautiful even in its vacancy, with tapered fingers
that try to play a piano when I slide my hand inside.
Will I ever be this graceful?

Upstairs, a sewing machine whirrs
and Mama calls my name:
Look what I've made for you.
See how it flatters your shape?

IN MY MIRROR

She glints along the beveled edge,
smiling and pressing her hand to the glass.

I touch her nose. She tips her head.
I lean close and feel her heat
flutter beneath my skin.

But, you're not real, I say,
and she says,
Of course I am

and slips behind
the curtain of my breath.

Under Anesthesia I Remember
a Watermelon with Slippery Seeds

Children again, we sit on our stoop and spit seeds
        into the tall grass.

We spit them across the lawn
            all the way to our father's garden shed.

My sister says
       This is how we grew.

Pulp clings to our fingers.
          Bumblebees tangle in our hair.

My lips form a whistle
       and seeds pelt the fevered sky.

Somewhere from our future, a surgeon says
       God what a mess.

His voice rumbles in the shed
       and a lawnmower lets out a roar.

Crickets shriek up from the chickweed—
         Petals swirl through linoleum halls.

Quick, my sister says, *do this*
       and spits seeds into her fist.

One by one we polish them.

ABOUT THE AUTHOR

Jackie Craven has recent poems in *AGNI, New Ohio Review, The Massachusetts Review, Pleiades, Ploughshares, River Styx,* and other journals and anthologies. She's the author of *Secret Formulas & Techniques of the Masters* (Brick Road Poetry Press) and a chapbook, *Our Lives Became Unmanageable* (Omnidawn), winner of the Omnidawn Fabulist Fiction Award. After earning a Doctor of Arts in Writing from the University at Albany, NY, she worked for many years as a journalist covering architecture, visual art, and travel. Visit her at JackieCraven.com

ACKNOWLEDGEMENTS

Columbia Poetry Review:
"Boys Scuttle Between the Walls," originally titled, "Boys Infest Our Building"

Columbia Poetry Review:
"Our House Is Menstruating," originally titled, "My House Is Menstruating"

Pleiades:
"She Never Answers My Knock,"
"Every Day, Her Steel Frame Expands,"
"She Tries to Hide the Oily Scent of Her Maturation,"
and "No One Speaks of the Empty Ghosts in the Basement Closet"
are expanded from a single short poem titled "Cyborg Sister"

Pleiades:
"Quietly at the Top of the Stairs," originally titled, "The Mystery at the Moss-Covered Mansion"

Poet Lore:
"Wings Throb Overhead," originally titled, "First a Throb of Wings"

Poets Reading the News:
"A Tadpole Gets in the Municipal Pool," originally titled, "Woozy in the Pool at Mar-a-Lago at 7:00 A.M."

Rogue Agent:
"Under Anesthesia I Remember a Watermelon with Slippery Seeds"

South Florida Poetry Journal:
"BuzzFuse Lists the World's Most Extraordinary Women"

Speculative North:
"Cyborg Sister" (short poem, reprinted from *Pleiades)*

50-Word Stories:
"Quietly at the Top of the Stairs," (reprinted from *Pleiades)*

Headmistress Press Books

Tender, Tender - Jessica Jewell
A Trickle of Bloom Becomes You - Jen Rouse
Cyborg Sister - Jackie Craven
Demoted Planet - Katherine Fallon
Earlier Households - Bonnie J. Morris
The Things We Bring with Us: Travel Poems - S.G. Huerta
The Water Between Us - Gillian Ebersole
Discomfort - Sarah Caulfield
The History of a Voice - Jessica Jopp
I Wish My Father - Lesléa Newman
Tender Age - Luiza Flynn-Goodlett
Low-water's Edge - Jean A. Kingsley
Routine Bloodwork - Colleen McKee
Queer Hagiographies - Audra Puchalski
Why I Never Finished My Dissertation - Laura Foley
The Princess of Pain - Carolyn Gage & Sudie Rakusin
Seed - Janice Gould
Riding with Anne Sexton - Jen Rouse
Spoiled Meat - Nicole Santalucia
Cake - Jen Rouse
The Salt and the Song - Virginia Petrucci
mad girl's crush tweet - summer jade leavitt
Saturn coming out of its Retrograde - Briana Roldan
i am this girl - gina marie bernard
Week/End - Sarah Duncan
My Girl's Green Jacket - Mary Meriam
Nuts in Nutland - Mary Meriam & Hannah Barrett
Lovely - Lesléa Newman
Teeth & Teeth - Robin Reagler
How Distant the City - Freesia McKee
Shopgirls - Marissa Higgins
Riddle - Diane Fortney
When She Woke She Was an Open Field - Hilary Brown

A Crown of Violets - Renée Vivien tr. Samantha Pious
Fireworks in the Graveyard - Joy Ladin
Social Dance - Carolyn Boll
The Force of Gratitude - Janice Gould
Spine - Sarah Caulfield
I Wore the Only Garden I've Ever Grown - Kathryn Leland
Diatribe from the Library - Farrell Greenwald Brenner
Blind Girl Grunt - Constance Merritt
Acid and Tender - Jen Rouse
Beautiful Machinery - Wendy DeGroat
Odd Mercy - Gail Thomas
The Great Scissor Hunt - Jessica K. Hylton
A Bracelet of Honeybees - Lynn Strongin
Whirlwind @ Lesbos - Risa Denenberg
The Body's Alphabet - Ann Tweedy
First name Barbie last name Doll - Maureen Bocka
Heaven to Me - Abe Louise Young
Sticky - Carter Steinmann
Tiger Laughs When You Push - Ruth Lehrer
Night Ringing - Laura Foley
Paper Cranes - Dinah Dietrich
On Loving a Saudi Girl - Carina Yun
The Burn Poems - Lynn Strongin
I Carry My Mother - Lesléa Newman
Distant Music - Joan Annsfire
The Awful Suicidal Swans - Flower Conroy
Joy Street - Laura Foley
Chiaroscuro Kisses - G.L. Morrison
The Lillian Trilogy - Mary Meriam
Lady of the Moon - Amy Lowell, Lillian Faderman, Mary Meriam
Irresistible Sonnets - ed. Mary Meriam
Lavender Review - ed. Mary Meriam

Made in the USA
Columbia, SC
18 February 2022